Life Through Lasagna Eyes

Samantha Kendall

D1456613

Publisher: PIAOTT Publishing LLC. Chicago, IL

Life Through Lasagna Eyes

Samantha Kendall

Printed in the United States of America

© 2012 by Library of Congress Cataloging-in-Publication Data

ISBN: 978-0-692-59903-7

0-692-59903-7

Photography by: Rodney Friend - SMP

PIAOTT
PUBLISHING
A Limited Liability Company

A Special Adoration to God

… For being my friend. Thank you for being here for me and carrying me through tragedy, hurt, heartbreak and pain. … For loving me when I barely loved myself. … For Your sense of humor, YOU really know how to make me laugh. … For giving me the passion for lasagna and pasta and blessing me to fall in love with it, Life Through Lasagna Eyes!

I Adore You!

I am grateful for Your Heart, Thoughts, and Your Love!

I remember you telling me, "I gotch u"!

You are my Daddy and I love you

Muah!

Dedication

I dedicate Life Through Lasagna Eyes in memory of my late daughter Amanda Skie Gallon, "Be Excited Mom" she always said, "God has big big big plans for you." Amanda was not only my daughter, but also a friend and I am thankful to God for blessing me to be her mother. I also dedicate this labor of love to her brothers, Mason and Maurice II, and her sister Morgan. We will forever love Amanda.

Acknowledgements

Thank you to Morgan, Mason, and Maurice II, family and friends for every encouraging word. To my cousin Bridgette Wright, my friend Felicia Benton, owner of PIAOTT Publishing LLC and Leslie, thank you for putting words into action. Pastors Victor and Gayla Walker (Pastor Papa and Mama), New Kingdom Christian Center, Bellwood, IL; I thank God for your wisdom and believing in me when others doubted. Pastor Bucky and Sandi Kerr, River of Life Church in Clarendon Hills, IL; when I was homeless and needed to get away, you opened your home to me and I will always be grateful. Pastors John and Elisa Veal, I thank God for your wisdom.

Stephen A. Martin, and Herbert R. Henderson of SMH2 Consulting, LeBron Dudley and Kenneth Williamson; thank you for being a friend and praying and believing in me.

Love you, Sammy!

Table of Contents

Adoration to My Heavenly Father
Dedications
Acknowledgements

Preface: The Day No Music Played   11
Chapter One: Life in the Noodle!   17
Chapter Two: The Meat: Loss & Love   29
Chapter Three: The Sauce!   41
Chapter Four: Recipes: Everything
                    In Between   51
Chapter Five: More Cheese Please!   61
Chapter Six: The Spices:
                    All My Children   69
Chapter Seven: The Baking Process:
                    Laughter   79
Chapter Eight: The Ouie Gouie:
                    Loving Again   87

Afterword   97
Index   101
Recipes From The Heart   107

The day no music played....

I have always been the sort of person who enjoys good music. Since I was a little girl — listening to Stevie Wonder and The Jackson 5 or songs like "Rubberband Man" and "This Little Light of Mine." The music made me feel like everything is possible!

Music is something we all enjoy! Rather its song's similar to, "Happy" by Pharrell Williams or "Cryin" by Aerosmith, there are songs that are universal and helps us out of our seat to dance. It is contagious, now everybody is dancing. I love the way some music encourages, inspires, and ignites me to dance, but it is chilling when the music stops playing in your life!

As I grew up to an adult, music continued to be instrumental in my life. However, one day it stopped playing and turned into silence.

It was February 14, 2006, Valentine's Day. It is a day when many people express their love for one another with candy, balloons, flowers and more.

I was preparing and packaging my product to be delivered to a customer. My oldest daughter, Amanda Skie Gallon (18), asked me if she could go out for Valentine's Day with her friends. We debated about a separate subject and then I gave her my permission to go enjoy herself.

My youngest daughter and I loaded the vehicle for the lengthy drive on the Chicago's Dan Ryan Expressway. Upon making the delivery, the customer and I chatted for a moment, then my daughter, Morgan, and I headed home.

On our way to the house, a feeling washed over me and I told my daughter that we needed to pray. I was not sure of what to pray for, so we prayed in general during the ride. When we arrived at our house, Amanda's best friend was waiting, upset, and crying. With a weeping voice, she told me that Amanda had been shot and is at Loyola Hospital.

I ran into the house to make an important call and drove to the hospital. When we got there, Amanda was in surgery. At this point, all I could do was wait for other family members and close friends to arrive.

The music that played within my heart stopped. Several thoughts ran through my mind as I waited to be called to the floor where my daughter was having surgery.

I distinctly remembered the security guard because it was her first night on duty and she wept so much for our pain. As we waited and prayed in silence, a nurse approached to escort us to the surgical waiting area. As we entered the elevator, we came upon a couple headed to the delivery room on the same floor but in the opposite direction. I turned my attention to how her husband remained calm during her labor pains when the elevator doors opened. It was the loudest sound I had ever heard.

As we walked out of the elevator, the Lord whispered to me, "It's okay." I heard it again, "It's okay." I knew immediately what that meant. As parents, however, we try to do whatever we can for our children; so I went to a washroom and kneeled to pray and the Lord told me to get up, "It's okay." As I tried to pray, the prayer would not lift off my back.

People have often said, "The prayer would not lift from my back, etc." and I never knew what that meant until experiencing it. Literally, no matter what I said, my words stood still. The Lord said, "Get up, it's okay." At that moment, getting off the floor from the knelt position was the longest journey to stand up.

Not long after entering the waiting room, the surgery ended. The doctor and nurses could not hold their emotions. They said, "We tried, but the bullet ricochet after entering her back and hit several vital areas and we could not stop the bleeding." The doctors, surgeons, and nurses were the most humane individuals I had ever seen.

They offered for family and friends to view Amanda. A few people wanted to see her, but the others were in shock. It was too much for them to handle. When I went to her, the doctor and nurses eyes became drenched from tears as I fixed Amanda's eyebrows. There were many things she loved, first and foremost being her Rock-A-Wear gear (that was her Prada). However, she always fussed over her eyebrows.

Amanda is/was a gorgeous young woman, and I wanted to make sure her eyebrows were fixed as I looked at her and said, "Goodbye." Sound no longer had a voice; I stood still while everyone around me moved in what seem to be faster than normal.

February 14, 2006, was the longest night of my life. I somehow appeared sitting in her bedroom with an empty quietness. Music now undressed; finding harmony empty in my heart was gone. After countless hours, I recall having to make phone calls to her brothers Mason and Maurice II, paralyzing them into disbelief of a horrible reality.

The day the music stopped is when my heart got broken;
I felt abandoned, betrayed, unloved, and not wanted. The
thought of music did not enter my mind. My heart was
gutted, stepped on, ran over by a bus, and left on the ground
for anyone to walk on by my now ex-husband. Now, my oldest
daughter Amanda Skie Gallon was murdered. The final
remains of my heart sunk deeper into the pit of no return,
but God rescued me. He carried me through the darkness of
heartache and indescribable pain.

Though my ex-husband broke his covenant with God and
with me, I forgave him for abandonment and breaking my
heart. I also was able to forgive the man that viciously
murdered my daughter.

Through the power of forgiveness and prayer, I became
free from the bondage of hurt and pain. ... And the music
played again.

A Lesson Learned

A recipe is a set of instructions for preparing a particular
dish, including a list of ingredients required. A recipe, like
life, provides you guidelines and a list of steps to help along
the way. You crawl before you walk; you drink milk before you
can eat steak.

Each layer in Life Through Lasagna Eyes provides life recipes needed to encourage, unfold, or help you wherever you are during the process of discovering you!

Lasagna is much like life! You got the base noodle that provides the strength and solidity. Much like lasagna, life is layered with passion, goodness, sticky stuff, and another noodle of stability. That layer is then covered by and topped off with specialty sauce.

Now with lasagna, sometimes, the ingredients in the middle makes little sense, but the finished product results into something amazing. For me, that is what life is like. Lasagna with eyes, there is a balance! It is the ability to look through a different lens and visualize your passion. A kid once asked me if lasagna had eyes. "Can it see?" he questioned. I thought to myself, hmmm. I chuckled with a smile and said, "Not eyes like you and I, but another set of eyes that can provide love, warm smiles, and happiness."

My journey of becoming a lasagna expert began with life's loss, tragedy, triumph, and love. And here is where Life Through Lasagna Eyes begins!

Chapter One

Life in the Noodle!

Recipe #1 - Don't Settle for Misery Living,

Find Yourself – Find You!

*L*asagna (also lasagne) is an Italian dish consisting of this pasta baked with meat or vegetables, cheese, and sauce.

Lasagna supplies nutrients to athletes, trainers and is a calorie-dense food that may be helpful for bodybuilding, depending on the goals. The pasta in lasagna is delicate with a pleasant flavor and provides the base and stability to hold up and seal the other ingredients.

The heart of the matter through passion, love, and prayers supplies stability of strength in your journey. Sometimes we do not always get the right measurements when cooking. Perhaps it is having all the ingredients needed but the amount used is incorrect or substituting all the ingredients measured. Gosh darn, it came out lumpy! Like the lasagna noodle, it provides strength and steadiness.

When dealing with life's many layers, events may consist of pleasantness and great joy or pain, despair, hurt, or something I call the silent hurt. The silent hurt, to me, is the one that can almost take its victims out. It is an indescribable feeling, not having anyone to talk to. Especially when this forced solitude is based on people's proven judgments during simple conversations.

When things like that happen, many people may choose to suffer in silence. This is what I call the silent hurt. Stay away from it because, like the cheese that melts between the layers of lasagna; it oozes on everything it touches.

The cheese in the lasagna holds things together like the encouragement of good friends in your life. Stay open to your friends. Do not let the silent hurt cover your life.

One challenging layer in my life was when I came home from work one day and my ex-husband was gone.

Well, son of a grits and biscuit! Ironically, that day, we were scheduled to move. The interesting part is that I had just spoken with him before entering our townhouse. He asked if I made it to the house yet. I said, "No." "Okay, call me when you do," he said. We chatted briefly about other things as usual. Nothing seemed strange.

So upon discovering he was gone, I made babysitting arrangements, picked up the scheduled U-Haul, and moved in the rain. I remember thinking, "How awesome is destiny's beginning, and gosh, those cupcakes from a local convenient store I had afterward was the best I ever had."

During this layer, I had a lot to deal with all at once, covered with emotions of being betrayed. Funny, though, I remember bathing later that night and having so much peace; A peace I cannot explain. The entire time I was in the tub, I kept thinking that I had the best treat ever waiting for me! I said to myself, "What a way to end that relationship, with a damn good cupcake."

Heartbreak is the worst, especially when a silent intruder insidiously invades the heart. You have to dig deep and remember that destiny and some great cupcakes are waiting for you!

Just think. This type of abandonment is a blessing. It hurts but do not settle in the misery of someone else's deceit. A bridge had been long built and lit up for you. Everything underneath it cannot touch you.

Several months later, my oldest daughter, Amanda, was murdered. The grief of a failed marriage shifted to the tragic death of my daughter.

Doing something differently turned out to be therapeutic while mourning the death of Amanda and the pain that followed. I decided that if anyone asked me how I was doing, I would tell him or her how. So, if I was sad, I expressed it instead of saying, "Fine," and holding everything inside.

By doing this, I learned that many people all around are willing to listen. Even if it is for a few minutes, it proved to be a therapy during my process.

When a tragedy of this size strikes, your family and friends become sensitive to what you are experiencing. You may not hear much from them and when you do, it may not be when you want. They too are in a state of shock and dealing with the hurt in their own way.

Sometimes, just knowing that they will be there in your time of grief helps you greatly during this difficult process. There is a strength that comes with this pain; an inner strength that God gives to sustain, reinforced by those that love and care for you. Your friends and family are like the cheese in lasagna; holding everything together.

In the midst of my deepest pain and hurt, I decided if anyone should ask me how I was doing, I was going to answer their question honestly. One day, shortly after laying Amanda to rest, I was preparing to go to the grocery store.

That morning, I went to the washroom in starting the day and looked at my toothbrush.

I reached to grab it and boy was it heavy. This toothbrush felt like it had the weight of a large hammer. Applying the toothpaste was not much different. Nonetheless, it took a long time to get ready, but eventually I was able to begin the day. I needed to buy important items from a well-known grocery store.

Getting there seemed like a road trip in itself. I entered the store in what appeared to be slow motion while others around me were on fast forward. Hours later, I arrived at the checkout line and the cashier asked me how I was doing. I expressed that my daughter had been murdered and described the pain. She listened. I walked away in a better state of mind than when I entered the grocery store.

What a wonderful day it turned out to be. I smiled, mostly forced. I thought to myself, it has to get a little better each day over time.

I kept in the forefront of my mind what Amanda always told me. "Do you Ma, move forward, God has big big big things for you." As painful as it was, I did and moved forward.

At first, it did not seem right since she was not here anymore. But, my gratefulness to God for allowing me to be her mother and friend, and keeping her cherished in my heart always was the ingredients needed.

The moving forward process became part of the base of the noodle in my life's lasagna. This is the noodle that provided the foundation and soundness needed for building the unique layers of the future.

A foundation is the lowest load-bearing part of a building typically known as the ground level. In this case, of course, we are talking in terms of lasagna and the pan holding the pasta is the base, but the bottom noodle is what holds all the other layers together once taken out the pan. This noodle provides the groundwork to building unique lasagnas and carries the weight despite the complexity of ingredients. Metaphorically, the bottom noodle is the underlying principle or the starting point of your life's lasagna.

Moving forward can be scary and a hard thing to do especially being unaware of the future.

Doing it immediately may seem strange, but oftentimes if you linger, eventually you will be forced to deal with the pain rather your ready or not.

No two days are alike when dealing with the loss of a child. It is physically and mentally exhausting.

During this journey, I met two doctors, Dr. Dennis Nwachukwu and Dr. Robert Miller at Loyola Family Center in Maywood, Illinois. They always have an encouraging word regardless if you there for sinus issues or an annual physical check-up.

One day I visited Dr. Nwachukwu for a yearly physical, he asked me how I was doing. I spoke quietly and said, "I'm going to be okay. I hurt and hurt, but I'm going to be okay." He then said to me "the brain is powerful."

As strange as it may seem, I knew exactly what Dr. Nwachukwu was saying. He was talking about training your brain. Something I will talk more about in the next chapter.

Now you know strength is in the base noodle! Like layers that include helping others, trust and happiness, strength is needed to deal with false friends to discovering who you are and loving again.

One of my callings is lasagna. It took moving forward (the words of my late daughter Amanda) to discover it! Where are you in your life's lasagna? Is it the base, the mixture in between, or all over the place?

Determining where you are in your lasagna, whether it is the pain losing a child, separation, divorce, a bad break-up, low self-esteem, or heartbreak, you can discover your passion, or more importantly, you can find YOU!

Story: Feeling Pretty!

A little dark skinned girl is all I was in the sight of those around me. "Hey, blackie! Need an eraser?" Well, you can see where that was going.

Growing up, I do not remember ever feeling pretty, but my birthday photos indicated otherwise. Looking at one picture, I began to read it differently.

It was a cool evening where the breeze was easy with the linen blanketed sun. The dinner dishes were washed and put away. My brother, sister, and I took turns to bathe and get ready for bed. When I was all ready to slumber for the night, I prayed for the first time as I remember. I was not quite sure of what it was, but I detailed my prayer and asked God for a yellow dress.

Clean cut and sharply dressed is how our mother clothed us. So, when I prayed that particular night, I kneeled on my knees, clasped my hands together, closed my eyes, and rested my forehead against my hands. I said, "God, can you put a yellow dress in my closet tomorrow, it has flowers on it and shiny?"

I walked over to the window lit with the moon's radiance located next to the closet door and looked up as though I was solidifying my prayer.

The next morning I anxiously ran to the deep closet and saw no dress. Hopeful, I told myself that when I got home from school, it would be there! After a few days of running to the closet to no avail, one day, it was there. Excited and beaming with happiness, I felt like the prettiest girl on the block. I did not know the meaning of prayer, but something happened when I did. It became my foundation to lay things on. With prayer, you do not have to carry them.

Much like the lasagna noodle being the base that holds all the ingredients and everything in between the layers, prayer is the groundwork for stability. It had become an important part of my life; coupled with building a relationship with the Lord.

Like telling Him good morning and the love I have for Him and thanking Him for being my Daddy. Having foundation brings meaning to your life.

Your greatest pain is not an Anchor!
Samantha Kendall

You are a winner! Settle for what?

Chapter Two
The Meat: Loss & Love

Recipe #2 — Train Your Brain, Be Determined!

*n*aturally, when we lose something or someone, we shift instantly to a feeling of grief. Like losing a loved one or when your dog dies, darn, it hurts! The loss of a job or being passed over for a promotion you have long since waited for can be devastating. Someone you love abandons you without warning; your spouse has an affair and leaves you. Loss can leave its victims in despair, but know victory awaits you.

Finding yourself is an amazing discovery in your journey. During times of loss, you can tap into the strength, love, integrity, and compassion in the many layers inside your innovation in life's lasagna.

This is what I call the meat in lasagna. It deals with the heart of the manner — loss and love. Loss and love always turn into a tug-of-war. Finding the strength to move forward after a loss is difficult, like meat, it is a source of nourishment necessary for growth. The meat in life's lasagna becomes a source of strength that is beneficial in nourishing life's existence. Now the meat can be anything from Ground Turkey to Brussels Sprout. Looking through Lasagna Eyes, adding the pain of your loss and the love you shared is meat between the layers.

The way you think in life's lasagna is cultivating as you look through the lens of self-discovery.

Conditioning your brain from dealing with loss and shifting to a different lens may seem passive. In life's lasagna, I found that the meat in the layer fostered the strength I needed to smile, believe in love again, and embrace my passion. Getting there was not as hard as one may think; it happened when I changed the lens.

In grieving the loss of a relationship or the loss of a loved one, remembering significant moments that brings a smile to your face is evidence of the meat in your life's lasagna. With a different lens, forward movement involves nurturing your passion. There will be challenges along the way. Looking through your life's lasagna lens will allow you to build extraordinary layers. The lens triggers the brain to feed on positive thoughts and be laser focused. In this discovered layer, there is no room for negativity.

It was not until one cool summer day in Chicago that my eyes were unlocked from the mask it wore. The air was kind and moved gently as I stood at a bus stop on Madison.

There, an older gentleman, old enough to be a grandfather walked near me and said, "Good afternoon young lady." I repeated the same instead calling him, "Sir" and smiled. Sir walked past but turned back. The alcohol reeked from the pores of his skin and I held my nose inwardly to avoid it, but it was far too strong.

He said, "Young lady, you smile, but there is so much sadness in your eyes. Eyes always tell the truth." I could not look his way because I knew Sir was right. My eyelids got heavy, and I blinked slower.

This was the A-Ha moment for me. Although I was looking through a different lens, my eyes were filled with pain. I wept much when I arrived at my residence and knew it was time for me to open my natural eyes in Life Through Lasagna Eyes!

The meat layer in lasagna is equivalent to our natural eye, which is the organ of vision. The eye is connected to the brain through the optic nerve. Experiments according to an article on the Scientific Psychic website have shown that the back of the brain maps the visual input from the eyes.

The brain contains the input of our two eyes into a single three-dimensional image (let's call this passion, purpose, and position through lasagna eyes).

It is important to know that our focus begins with a vision. When you discover your passion, your vision becomes crystal clear. Let us build!

Like pages, you turn when reading books; it is layered! The movies you watch; it is layered! Lasagna; it is layered! Each layer will unfold your vision and postures you to focus.

Although you may have experienced trauma, tragedy, loss, or anything that causes severe anguish know that each day is going to get better. The visional focus, everything you discover about the love in your loss and the nurturing love is the meat in life's lasagna.

During the meat layer, I encouraged my passion ignited through food by expressing my love for family, friends, others, and myself. So, I cooked and studied lasagna with the music blasting in the background with joy. So much joy that all my neighbors could hear. I danced while cultivating my passion too.

Although, I could never figure out that fancy steppers move, I danced and danced. Dance anyone?

The meat in life's lasagna helps you develop, support, and raise the layer you are building. Taking you to heights, you have never imagined. On the other side of love is loss. Although loss hurts and we may misunderstand it, know that something greater is to come. I, in no way, make light of any pain you're feeling or may have felt, but I know through loss and love, forgiving yourself prepares you to build greater on the next layer. Once you turn on your passion, you cannot turn it off.

The meat in life's lasagna allowed me to create and originate layers. Layers like loss and love, finding your passion and maturing it. Placing your likes and dislikes in this layer combines many flavors like meat or vegetables.

Not everyone likes asparagus (I love it!), but when fused with other ingredients, it becomes the star ingredient between the layers.

Take yourself, for example, you have experienced loss — place it in the layer; now mix it with forgiveness, love, your laughter, and purpose; you are well on your way to building upon your passion and welcoming the next layer to build the next big thing.

Positioning the meat is intentional in constructing the next big thing. Thanks to my good friends Herbert R. Henderson and Stephen A. Martin owners at SMH2 Consulting, I learned positioning the ingredients is strategic. Have you ever eaten lasagna that was more like a soup with meat or dry like bread (A-ha)?

The position in your passion and purpose is important and should be a star of strategy in your journey. Now I am, not talking about titles we have, but in which something is placed or arranged.

Story: Lose Negativity!

When you undo something, you cancel it out; reverse it. Undoing involves defeating it!

For 12 years, she was advised to go to school, work, and get a job. "If you don't do that, find a man and become his whore. He will take care of you."

"I hate girls, basically, I hate you!" "You will never be anything, you can't own a business; you're not smart enough."

Needless to say, the list goes much further. In my opinion, individuals that reflect these attitudes to their children or other people have a lifeless mindset.

To hear on daily that you will never be anything is a lie! Do not allow anyone to ever lure you into his or her negative mindset. If this is you and all that is played in your subconscious is negativity, let your thoughts be louder than their voice!

Think aloud and drown the voice of naysayers no matter who it is.

Rather you are bathing, sleeping, eating, or dancing with negativity, do not allow it to out-speak the thought God gave you to think.

With your mindset crushing the voice of negativity, you undo the perpetual bad habits of their life's choices. Negativity is a form of control and if you allow, it will penetrate your mind and ultimately control every move you make.

This is what some people do in relationships to mask their insecurities. I will expound more on my next book, They Ain't Gon See You Comin!

The mind is powerful. Muting negativity after being mistreated, can lead your thoughts and ideas into infinity.

Negative people are the first to notice greatness and success in your life. It is clear evidence that your thoughts are powerful. Regardless of their efforts, the result of not allowing unfocused individuals to determine who you are is your success! So laugh aloud — they cannot anchor you. You are the winner!

Finding your passion unfolds its future!

Samantha Kendall

Enjoy the quiet times...
There holds your strength!

Chapter Three

The Sauce!

Recipe #3 — Enlarge Your Life! Add to it!

Feel Normal Again!

A good chef knows that sauce is the star to complete an entrée. Ever gone to a barbecue and there was no sauce; Pizza with no sauce; Turkey with no gravy; Lasagna with no sauce; Ice Cream with no chocolate sauce?

The sauce is synonymous to feeling good. In the discovery of your passion, there is the A-Ha moment that makes you feel complete. When it comes to the sauce, sometimes no entrée is needed. To put it simply, it is pleasurable to taste just by dipping your finger in it and enjoying Mmm!

The sauce is steady. It provides flexibility to the noodle, adding life to it and allowing the natural taste to emerge. While creating your sauce, you feel alive in the A-Ha moment and no one can take that away from you.

Assembling requires the entire you, but the base, life in the noodle, and the sauce will always support your passion, purpose, and who you are! For instance, in the layers on top of the sauce, you can add the bitterness you once felt and balance it with forgiveness.

Now you can build on top of the sauce. You can add hate and balance it with love.

I threw my whole self in lasagna. Picture yourself swimming with joy, laughing, being strengthened, dancing, and loving in your passion. I saw Life Through Lasagna Eyes! … And it saw me!

The sauce is not complete with just tomatoes; other ingredients are needed to expand the taste. These ingredients are all of the accomplishments you have made. When tragedy or heartbreak hits, it subtracts ingredients in your life, leaving you to feel empty and lopsided.

Hold on, its time to enlarge your life!

Your journey's ingredients are to help you discover yourself and your passion. Filter the pain and dance. Seriously! Yes, now! When I did it, I laughed to myself saying, "What a goofy move, but hot grits and potatoes, it feels good to dance like this." The goofier, the better! Release some of the tension so you can focus on the structure of your sauce.

The framework of filtering and enlarging your life begins with forgiveness. Forgive the person that crushed your heart. Forgive the person that murdered your child. Forgive the person that ruined your lawn. Forgive, forgive, forgive! Be strong and courageous.

In my case, forgiveness did not mean that memories of my child and moments I remembered when she was in the womb would not be there. The truth of the manner is the pain will always be there.

One way you can deal with it is through rediscovering and enlarging your life by finding your passion.

Pray and open up about where you are in life; begin a Non-for-Profit organization, start journaling, write a book, start a fund in your family that helps send your younger relatives to college, join a book club, embrace a new sport. These are just examples of how to enhance your journey. Be courageous like sauce! The sauce is bold when all the ingredients are blended together. Do not waste another moment in your grief, wipe your face, and get up from where you are!

Amanda's death was paralyzing. It made me numb. The problem was not being numb; it was when the numbness wore off. Like Novocain at a dental office, once it wears off, the excruciating pain hits you like a ton of bricks. You are more sensitive to the inexpressible pain. Heartbreak can shock your system into a paralyzed state to which would also, at some point, wear off.

The sauce is amazing in assuring that something great will follow your pain. You have much to look forward to. There is success and feeling normal again, or even falling in love. The sauce is solid. It does not matter the entree it tops; it is the sauce. Enlarging your life compliments a healthy and humble mindset. Once you have forgiven, its time to add to your life and expand.

If you are the owner of a large or small business, school administrator, teacher, professional sports player, houseparent, student, or entrepreneur, no matter your occupation, make bigger where you are and think great.

Think Great! Thinking greater enlarges and adds to your mental and physical position.

Where you are headed is much more extraordinary than your current circumstance. Changing your mindset is as critical as drinking water or getting up to brush your teeth! The moment you are in right now is not to be compared to your destiny! Get up and do it now! Think great!

Story: I Can't Stop!

My emotions overflowed dampening the sound of my voice. Amanda had been buried and I was thick with aches and pain in places I did not know could hurt.

As the numbness wore off, there was no over the counter medicine I could take for this pain.

I needed to get away and fast so, I went to a park and sat on a bench. There was a school near the park. The children were in recess. I watched them play and thought about my children when they were younger. It brought back good memories. It wasn't until the school's recess was over that a little boy was swinging on a swing.

All the children had lined up and entered the school building. Not this little one, he continued to ride the swing. His teacher noticed he was missing and came back outside and called his name to come back in the building.

He yelled, "I Can't, I Can't Stop! I Can't Stop!" I laughed hard; he could not stop the swing from swinging. His teacher was laughing too as she ran over to help him out of the swing.

I thanked God for that laugh. It was exactly what I needed! God knows how to make us laugh or draw our attention off pain and hurt. At that moment, my tears turned to laughter and more laughter. That was the start of me learning to laugh all over again. Even now when I think about it, I laugh!

Putting all of yourself in your passion is what it takes. Ever heard the statement - I have to laugh to keep from crying? Many people have said this at one point or another. But if you choose to cry because laughing hurts too much, that is also ok.

When building upon your passion, like lasagna, the sauce stage is when you overcome all odds and enlarge your life!
Samantha Kendall

Feeling nothing at times is normal.
In the morning, you will know what to do!

Chapter Four
Recipes: Everything In Between

Recipe #4 — Do Something Nice for Others!

Say, "Thank You!"

A recipe is a formula with instructions or process…a guideline. With every recipe comes excitement from purchasing the ingredients to completing the task for you to enjoy with family, friends, or yourself. This burst of energy follows as you obtain the necessary ingredients.

No one knew that I was sleeping on my bedroom floor. I love pillows, so they were placed everywhere. Several comforters were underneath for extra comfort after a long day of making deliveries. Deliveries of my lasagna were made from one end of town to the other on public transportation coupled with cab rides. A few hours of sleep was stolen, and deliveries would be made all over again.

My landlord at the time was watching me; I did not know he paid that much attention. However, he stopped by to repair my washroom sink that drained slowly or sometimes not at all.

Upon walking towards the washroom, he looked to the right in the direction of my bedroom and noticed I slept on the floor. I thought to myself, "Darn, I forgot to close the door." Well, it turned out not to be as embarrassing as I thought. It sparked a conversation.

I told him my story. The good, the bad, and how I believe in my passion and sacrificing for it. It provoked him to tears.

I never share my story to do such, but we are human and those that are real can attest when something tugs on their mind and heart.

His name is Kenneth Williamson. For a little while, he would notice me traveling early in the morning and coming back late at night. After a hard day of travel in Chicago's knee-deep snow, I looked forward to those comfy pillows and blankets. ... And I repeated this again and again and again.

One day, Kenneth called me, he said, "I would like to talk with you." "Okay, is everything all right," my reply. We went back and forth, as he assured me things were well. He was not trying to be nosey, but he expressed how it bothered him that I slept on the floor. My defenses kicked in to say, "I'll be okay." That was not good enough; he mentioned that since the Thanksgiving holiday is coming up, I would like to do something nice for you. I want to take you to pick out a bedroom set at The Room Place (Harlem Furniture Store).

This was such good news. You always hear of good deeds done. Or, you know of the ones you do in secret for others but never experience them yourself. I did not know how to react. At first, I thought, "Yea, Right" and soon found out he was serious.

Right before the holiday, we went shopping for my bedroom set – I had never had an entire set. "Oh! My goodness!" Being mindful, I picked out a set on sale and the mattresses were comfortable, stern, and durable.

A few weeks went by before delivery since it was on lay-a-way. The set has a black leather pillowed headboard, with dark brown trimmings with a dresser, mirror, nightstand, and lamps to accompany. It was the most beautiful bedroom set I had ever seen. I told Kenneth, thank you!

Often, your gratitude during the sleeping on the floor days determines a positive outcome. No one is above anyone being a blessing in their lives in any way, form, shape or manner. Someone that has, what some may think is everything, may need a meaningful conversation added to a materially empty life. Others might need a compliment. So, do something nice for others.

The main ingredients between the layers may be love, happiness, or an unselfish act that you do for someone else. Blending it all together is the formula for good friendships and the beginning of a happy life.

The ingredients you put between the layers is what makes the outcome even more exciting. Through Lasagna Eyes, I learned my ingredients included love, passion, and more love. Finding your life's passion after being beaten up with heartbreak and tragedy sounds much more easier than it actually is.

Loving again after heartbreak or opening your eyes and heart after the loss of a child is not about timing, but the process.

During my process, I thought about how loving and living again works! I thought about the words a young woman shared with me that held my daughter after being shot, she told me, "She asked for her mommy."

Tears flow in this memory. Laughing seemed wrong for me to do – I am still learning how! Placing those memories in your recipe allows love to surface.

I stayed busy for a long time and found that it was not the answer to healing. Ultimately, I crashed. BOOM! Is how it happened. I thanked God for carrying me in the midst of everything. I read the Bible, went for walks, listened to good music — jazz to gospel and everything else in between; Helped homeless people; Smiled, shared my story, listened to other people's stories, hugged people, and encouraged them.

Refreshed (revived, re-energized), I felt loved and thanked the Lord for loving me and showing me all types of favor.

Story: Doing Something Nice for Others!

During the early A.M. of the windy City, ice cycles were on viaducts, bridges, and vehicles. I picked up my son, Maurice II for campus and shared with him that I needed to make a stop before dropping him off at school. He said, "Kool."

He had no idea where we were going. The ride was conversational as he shared his aspirations and general talk. We arrived at the lower part of the Wacker Drive bridge that housed some of our city's homeless. While opening the door, I revealed my routine of providing a few meals to the homeless when my schedule permits. His eye lit up while saying, "Mom, that's Awesome." He went on to talk about how big my love was. He joined me in handing out meals. I talked to some of the people that lived there for the short term. I say temporarily because God can change their situation around, "Just Like That," in any moment. Everyone, there was grateful and thankful for the meal ...they had not enjoyed lasagna in a long time. May God bless them always!

Smile, someone is in your corner and

love is on your side!

Samantha Kendall

Pay it forward!
Pack an extra lunch for someone else.

Chapter Five
More Cheese Please!

Recipe #5 — "When Life Throws You a Lemon,
Your Melted Cheese is There!"

*T*he sticky stuff is all good! Often times, we need it to keep things together-melted cheese, this relates to the people in your life that hold things together during difficult times. There are always one or more people in our lives that is the cheese. Like lasagna, once the bare ingredients fuse together with the cheese and topped with sauce, it locks in the flavors so you can savor the taste in every bite. When life throws you a lemon, your melted cheese is there!

The cheeses in your life are your crusaders and will keep you encouraged. It is amazing how cheese seems to spread and forms a shape; sized just right for you. Therefore, like cheese, the people around you will be flexible and sensitive to your needs. They will be accommodating, much like the cheese in lasagna, a helpful part of the entrée.

With life's punches, it is easy to sink to not believing much. Your purpose is preserved and intentional for you! The things you may have considered bad or good — is going to work out for your good!

Something attractive happens when you believe. Your voice becomes a power tool. It speaks to your vision.

I made a faith jump in my passion for lasagna and landed on the deep water. I was skiing, sliding, walking, and running on and in it. My feet were soaked and wet. Starting a business is not a shallow water move.

Some people said I was crazy to jump into it so daringly, but my pioneers of encouragement praised it was the best move ever. Please, if you have any "Un-cheese" people in your life disguised "haters" and you want to move forward, tell them GOODBYE!

Part of believing in your discovered passion, purpose, and position is in your voice and eyes. Remember the focal point in eyes begins with the vision. I am talking about your belief in the expectation of GOOD news, GREAT news! Have you ever had on an interview for a contest, school, or job, only to find that you did not win or are accepted? Did you drown yourself in the why and/or why not?

Negativity is readily available and waiting for you to pick it up leaving the positivity dormant. I learned this when I entered several contests and was close, but did not win. I use to belittle the efforts I had made with doubt. Not anymore! I believe that if I had been expecting great news back then, the outcome would have been different.

To do the work required and not believe in its greatness is mute. It will not manifest! Every day you expect good news! I remember the Lord telling me once that I was going to hear bad news. What He said after that really astonished me. He said, "The bad news is in fact good news in reverse." Hallelujah, so not all bad news is bad.

Get rid of the old mindset of your past and/or present that was designed to keep you crippled into never discovering how powerful you are. You take on a new mindset with great news expectancy! Anticipating more replaces negativity and your faith is increased.

Say to yourself, "More cheese, please!" We can never get enough of great news and great people in our lives that will hold us together. So, believe right now that you will receive great news and expect it!

Story: Again, Please!

My niece Tiara resided with us for a while during the first four years of her life. Her mother had faced challenges that prohibited her to taking proper care of Tiara, so my ex-husband and I took her into our home.

Tiara arrived with her mother wrapped in a blanket with a diaper, socks, and t-shirt. We made all the necessary adjustments to care for her as our own.

When she was a little older, the movie Monster's Inc. was released and soon became available on DVD. We knew how much she loved the movie, so we purchased the DVD. Why did we do that? As little as she was, she had enough faith that if she said the words, "Play it!" She would watch the movie as many times as she wanted.

She was correct. Monsters Inc. played in our home every day and seemed like all day long it played. Instead of her saying, "More please!" She would repeat, "Again" and "Again." We just figured she would somehow get tired of the movie playing, but she never did.

Instead, she would hide her treats in the entertainment center so she would have something more to munch on during her "Again" episodes. She exercised her faith for great news by her words "Again."

Again equates to "Once more; Another time; Yet again; Over; Over Again; All over again; for a Second time."

We were happy to play it over and over, because of her faith and that it gave her much joy. The Lord has joy in doing great things for us over and over again because He loves us so much and our faith pleases Him.

Expect to have a great day!
Think Greater! Expect Greater!
Samantha Kendall

There is only one you! Be yourself.

Chapter Six
The Spices: All My Children

Recipe #6 — Let Memories Be Meaningful
Layers in Your Life!

*L*asagna is an entrée my children love. However, Amanda's favorite thing to eat was bacon and rice. Well, I could not compete with her favorite. I know that she loved my lasagna and would always say, "Do you Ma."

Amanda was born in Baltimore, Maryland on October 26, on my birthday. I was in labor for 72 hours and just knew that she would deliver before that. But on that day, the doctors eventually had to perform a C-Section due to the stress of being in labor for a long period.

When she arrived, I remember her lifting the top half of her body up with her hands as she looked at me. All I could do is smile. She was beautiful and both her hair and mines were everywhere.

I was not much of a beautician when it came to combing little girl's hair. "Yikes," I did not know what to do, but I learned by the time she was around 4 years old. I put her hair in two ponytail pompoms and voila, she had a style. I was proud of myself and learned much later how to style her hair beyond parting her hair in the middle.

Memories are another ingredient between the layers that helps us to heal more. When Amanda was a little girl, she never liked anything I cooked. Even if it was out of the can and I heated it up on the stove. She would cover her mouth and run (LOL!).

It was not until my Aunt Plumspy (Ann was her real name) shared with me that Amanda wanted real food, home cooked meals-southern style. Amanda responded with green lights to go ahead and eat. My daughter enjoyed soul food, southern, Italian and all other types of home cooked meals my aunt or the neighboring church would cook. After much trial and error on my end, I too learned how to cook southern meals.

Ironically, my aunt told me that I would be a great Chef one day and very successful in the industry. Wow! At the time, I could barely boil water for macaroni and cheese, among other dishes. But with much practice, I became a wonderful cook and later a great Chef. God knows what He has for us even before we know it and if we listen to people around us, He will tell you through them.

My aunt has since passed away and she was right. I found one of my passions in food. I fell in love with what God has for me through His Eyes – gourmet lasagnas.

Morgan and Mason, Amanda's twin siblings were born in May years later. Soon after, her youngest brother Maurice II was born during the same month. They simply adored Amanda. Amanda would often play church with her siblings and I could hear her telling them, "Say it louder; now jump; you're not jumping enough." It is the funny, meaningful, and personal memories that make the layers in your life more significant.

Candidly, when my children were younger, one of them thought every dish I made with meat was chicken. It was not until one day I prepared peppered steak and he said, "Mm-mm, Mom this is the best chicken in the world". Well, try convincing a 3-year-old that it is not chicken. I figured as long as he thinks it's all chicken. I will make liver and rice and watch what happens! As he grew older, he realized that it was different meats, but now we sure get a good laugh out of it.

One day, Amanda was getting ready for school and she was excited. It was a book festival at the private school she attended. I tended to Morgan, Mason, and Maurice II to take Amanda to school.

In one of our daily routines, her sister and brothers ate, played, took them for a walk, and napped; I received a phone call from Amanda's teacher. She expressed Amanda's excitement about the school's book festival. I said, "Great, I am glad that she enjoying herself".

Her teacher mentioned that she not only purchased books for herself, but she is buying books for all the students. "Did you give Amanda $100.00 dollars to purchase books Mrs. Kendall"? She asked. "No" I responded. After a moment of being a little mad, I could not help but smile about it. Knowing my daughter, she wanted people to learn more, Amanda wanted to help people. She had taken the money out of my purse and splurged on the students in her school buying them books to read.

Amanda loved her brothers and sister. There was nothing she would not do for them. Do not get me wrong; Amanda was tough but gentle like a butterfly and wise as a dove.

Her smile illuminated any room. She had a prophetic gift I respected. She would often tell me things and when it came to the past, she was not surprised because she was confident.

Amanda had this gift at an early age from birth. Her brothers and sister have the same and similar gifts.

She liked to climb trees; she loved cheesy puff chips and would have a fit in every store if we did not get her a bag before leaving the store. As she grew older, she developed her own fashion style. She loved Roc-A-Wear. She could sing. She was in ROTC. She played basketball in grammar and high school and our home was evident of her talent of braiding and styling hair by her many clients.

Amanda was quite the singer; she performed at the Washington School talent show at a young age and sang, "I'm Going Down" by Mary J. Bilge. She got a standing ovation. There's a part of the song that says, "What did I do wrong?" A few women from the audience waved their hands and said, "Nothing baby, you didn't do nothing, sang Mande!"

One time, Mason kept calling Amanda's name aloud during her kindergarten graduation. We really tried to keep him a quiet, but it did not work.

That was his way at an early age letting her know how happy he was for her. I think the cake he would enjoy after the graduation had something to do with it too!

See, it is those memories like that you cannot replace with anything else.

Memories are a part of healing. Embrace it. It took me a while before I could look at her photos because the pain was real. Remembering her laughter and love made it a little easier to look at pictures of her growing up.

Story: Morgan Hair on Fire!

During spring break, "All My Children" were at home while their dad and I went to work. Relax; they were old enough to be at home. Maurice II, who is an adult now, and I reminisced about the incident when his sister's hair caught on fire. Although this was no laughing manner at the time; you look back and it was quite funny; Like something out of the movies.

All of the children except Amanda were in the family room; she was near the kitchen. There was a candle lit on an end table, Morgan leaned back, and puff, her hair was on fire.

Maurice II said, "Morgan, your hair on fire." She said, "No it's not." Mason repeated saying, "Um Morgan, Yes it is, your hair on fire."

They went back and forth with chuckles in their voice, when Morgan ran to the washroom, Amanda running behind her screaming. Amanda washed her sister's hair after the repeat of screams back and forth — like a scene from a horror movie. Well, we got the phone call and got home as quickly as possible. All the children tried explaining the story and no two stories were alike. They were placed on punishment by their dad. The youngest took the blame. We took Morgan to the hospital. She was treated for an area on her scalp and recovered quickly.

Needless to say, her hair grew back beautifully. However, at the time, I am sure she did not appreciate going through her hair catching on fire. As I write this, I chuckle. At the end of the day, we knew we had each other; it turned our to be a great memory.

If your children run when you cook for them,
run with them!
Samantha Kendall

Your children are your greatest friends.
They know you inside and out!

Chapter Seven

The Baking Process: Laughter

Recipe #7 — Laugh Often!

A smile is as good as a laugh

*B*ubble, bubble, bubble the sound of laughter in life's lasagna. Once all the ingredients are layered in the pan, from loss and love to spices, its placed in the oven. Baking the lasagna has a sound like laughter. That laughter is the cheese and the sauce fusing the ingredients together to locking in its flavor. Once the cheese melts, you hear the sound of laughter!

Ever laughed so hard that your belly ached? Or laughed at someone else's laugh and no one could stop. Laughter can be impulsive, spontaneous or a funny thought stored in a compartment ready to erupt. It is similar to what happens when the ingredients in the baking process are blended.

During layers in building life's lasagna, I never thought I would laugh again. It became something I would watch other people do and wondered what the heck is wrong with them…they laugh too much! Well, needless to say, laughter turned out to be a bit more therapeutic than I thought.

Laughter feels good so why did I cheat it with sorrow? When sadness is done, it turns back into laughter.

Every time I tried to laugh, tears where the only thing that surfaced. I tried several times to laugh, but nothing happened so I began with tiny steps by smiling first — a smile is as good as a laugh.

Then I had chuckled gradually, but not gut wrenching laughter. I just figured that when something is funny, I would get my laughter back. In the meantime, smiling became my new laughter in the layers.

The laughter in this layer of life's lasagna is for enjoyment. Like a new addition to your family, the purchase of your new home, or sharing the stories of the day during family dinners. It is meant to be there to share in the joy of celebrated accomplishments.

Yes, I can eat this every day! In life's lasagna, this layer is about sharing. Share the moment when your baby takes his or her first step and the laughter of happiness spreads throughout your home. As you call your loved ones to share the news, life's lasagna is almost ready!

See, the laughter is the digger that goes deep into the root of your passion and promotes growth for your seed to grow.

With every chuckle, rather soft or heartfelt, your passion increases its strength igniting the roots within you to soar beyond heights you have ever imagined. I remember everything from creating the very first traditional lasagnas to creating exotic lasagnas beyond anything I could have ever envisioned.

My chuckles surfaced during the innovative process of blending various ingredients together, testing them out, and creating amazing lasagnas.

Create something miraculous by starting to laugh in your life's lasagna.

Story: The Day I Laughed!

Remember one of those moments that I stored the laugh in a compartment? My friend Felicia, owner of PIAOTT Publishing, and I were on our back from a Gluten Free Expo that Sam's Gourmet Lasagna exhibited. We talked about several things, but we mentioned our good friend LeBron "Lee" Dudley.

When I get excited, my voice raises and you do not see it coming. People that know me are fully aware and they usually brace themselves because it really is funny, but can be shocking to someone that has never experienced it; leaving their facial expressions frozen with their response to my excitement.

Well, I was sharing with Felicia that one day I got excited when I was talking with Lee. He turned his head away and said, "WTF is wrong with her." I remember the facial expression he made, and gutted a laugh while driving.

This laugh was so gutful that I almost had to pull over to let it all out. I knew the day would come when I would laugh again, but I did not expect it would be on the expressway I-94.

People in other vehicles literally heard me laughing since traffic was backed up, but steady. Felicia laughed too, but my laughter went on for a while. Tears drowned my face. I had to get air thus sticking my head out the window. The muscles in my stomach became tight; it felt so good though. So good to laugh again! After about 20 minutes of laughter, I shared with Felicia my struggle to laugh again since Amanda was murdered.

Some people may have heard me chuckle, but never like my laughter that I inherited from my Grandpa Eddie and his Pa-Pa and so on. He shared something with me one day when he heard me laugh as a little girl. He said, "You're gonna laugh so hard that you're gonna cut the cheese." Felicia said, "Thank you for sharing, and I'm glad I experienced seeing you laugh again." I am glad she was there too, because if I had continued laughing for another minute she would have needed to take the wheel. I am sure Felicia appreciated that I did not cut the cheese.

I am so glad I can laugh again! It feels really good!

Laughter is a Weapon... Use It!
Samantha Kendall

You will laugh again.

Chapter 8
The Ouie Gouie: Loving Again

Recipe #8 — Let It Happen

*T*he Ouie Gouie! That is the good loving you taste after the lasagna is removed from the oven. Like a hug from a good friend, the one you are in love with or having the courage to love again. The completed layers unfold full flavor in every bite and is cultivated with love, wholeness, and the courage to love again. Like the hug, arms open wide to embrace the one you love.

Loving again invites new possibilities of tasting love for the very first time or unfolding courage in every layer. Saying goodbye is never easy; rather it is to the death of a spouse, loved one or a broken relationship. Some goodbyes are well worth it; like the person that ripped your heart apart or abandoned you.

This type of goodbye is awesome. It welcomes learning more about yourself, forgiving others, as well as loving again. So there is some good in the bye!

Let love happen.

There was a man, let us call him Xavier. He would sit by the lake daily in the routine of his day adoring the scent and sight, remembering his late wife's perfume and the whisper of her love trying to muscle the strength to move forward.

It has been a while since she passed away and he was ready to love again. Approaching his favorite spot, he would loosen his tie, unbutton the top button of his ice blue and green shirt, cuff his brown suit jacket and sit until the sun rests for the day.

As he makes his way to his house a few blocks away, an immediate push shoves him forward giving him the courage to love again. He hears a whisper, "She's waiting on you." The tone thrusts him, with excitement; he readies himself to talk to her welcoming loving again.

Like Xavier, a person may lose their taste for loving again. Somehow, they manage to extract all their emotions blocking the flavor that love has to offer. Like lasagna in The Ouie Gouie, all the flavor including the love, joy, hurt and laughter is the taste. No one wants to eat lasagna where all the ingredients taste the same. This is much like Xavier's case before he decided he was ready to love again.

Understandably, when someone loses their spouse or the one they loved, it is natural to feel out of touch and grieve; maybe even becoming bitter.

That is not the resting place forever. Love is waiting on you just as fresh as when lasagna comes from the oven. Its ready to be enjoyed!

It is okay Ouie Gouie! Let love in... The Ouie Gouie was a challenging layer for me. I thought I did not know what loving again felt like so I closed the door on it. I toiled with the thought of loving again; running and hiding from it. I soon learned that you could not hide from love.

It was not until recently someone shared with me that I know what it feels like and it will manifest soon to say the least. So I related this information to knowing how to make lasagna strategically and enjoy it once it is all done.

It became simple to me that loving again is learning to say, "Hello!" It is hard to say hello to loving again if you never say goodbye.

Like the layers in previous chapters that involved saying hello to your passion to goodbye to "Un-cheesy" people, you can only enjoy The Ouie Gouie – the good stuff, when you enjoy every ingredient in the cooked lasagna.

With your new vision and passion, love is fresh and has endless possibilities. As I recall my late grandparents and the love they shared, it was endless. My Grandpa Eddie once told me the story of how he expressed his love for my late Grandma Bertha.

He visited my Great Grandparents and told them how much he loved Bertha and that he was going to marry her. Well, my Great Grandparents did not take kindly to that, but sure enough, they married and had 6 children and a host of grandchildren and great-grandchildren. When I was a little girl, my siblings and I would visit our grandparents on the weekends. With much anticipation, every Thursday could not bring Friday fast enough.

During our visit, we learned about fresh vegetables from my Grandma's homegrown garden. My grandmother made the best preserves from the apple and peach tree on their property. On Saturday mornings, we ate the best pancakes ever.

While visiting, I played sports and was quite the tomboy. More importantly, I recall the way my grandparents showed love for each another.

He would give her a kiss (as he would say, "Sum sugga") right in the middle of their conversation or they would give each other a loving pinch on the buttocks.

As kids, we giggled. I am so glad I witnessed their love and grew to understand that expressing your love plays a significant role in the relationship. That is just the beginning of The Ouie Gouie.

Story: Loving Again

I noticed his eyes glance the curves of my legs, as he would shadow the shoes I wore. He would look and then turn away looking at others around us. He cascaded the roundness of my face and looked at my eyes. Noticing the strength of his hands, kindled heart, gentle eyes... I enjoyed this occasion. Playing his game since he did not want me to know that I saw him was intriguing.

He looked at me as though he knew all about me. Time stood still and a few seconds seemed like forever relaxing in the strength of his eyes. I enjoyed this occasion. His stare and glance felt nice after a decade of waiting for the one. He was there to expand our love, ready to share his life with me.

I walked reminiscing in slow motion the movement of his eyes, detailing the length of his lashes and love in his heart as I approached my vehicle, paid for parking, picked up dinner, and drove to my house. I turned the key to my condominium and the blink of his eyes as he watched. I opened my door and he said, "I prayed to God and He answered me with you."

You see... the one could be around you the whole time...

Loving again means saying, "Hello!"

Samantha Kendall

Love has its own agenda, it does not ask for your permission!

Recipe: Life Through Lasagna Eyes!

Entrepreneurship is a great thing, stay consistent and on track. Forget the 40 hours a week! Follow your passion. If that is not a current option for you at this time, use the 40 hours as a stepping-stone. Do your passion and do it NOW! While you are on lunch — do your passion, while you on your break, do your passion! Have conference calls during your lunch or break. Make it happen... And know that as you are doing that, God has got your back, front, left, right and every part of your in between; He has you covered.

Prioritize your time and do not let anyone, and I mean ANYONE! Disengage you from the love and passion you have found. More importantly, you found you.

Do damage! Massively construct, then break it down, flush out, and continue to follow your passion until it's so embedded within you. Until it is married to you and you to it!

Many people lack the knowledge of how the brain works. Have successful thoughts! It is not necessarily about perseverance, your successful thoughts becomes the focal point and know that the Lord has great plans for you.

For I know the plans I have for you, "Declares the LORD," plans to prosper you and not to harm you, plans to give you hope and a future ~ Jeremiah 29:11. The Lord preserves you coming out of your situation and moving forward in a new direction! Psalms 121:8 "The LORD shall preserve thy going out and thy coming in from this time forth, and even forevermore."

Negativity is always available to you. My son Maurice II shared with me Earl Nightingale's quote, "Success is a progressive realization of a worthy idea." Once you have it and follow that, you will be successful. An idea and a thought are progressive.

Age does not retire you; your income retires you. Age has nothing to do with it. What people do with a billion dollar idea is turn it into a trillion dollar idea and retire. I am sure they got discouraged, but I believe they turned it into a positive.

Remember the monopoly game's Go! Every time you passed go, you obtained a certain amount of game money! Go and go pass Go! When the wheel of a vehicle turns, it moves forward constantly. The only time it rolls backward is if the driver shifts the gears. Allow your shifts to be used for reconstructing necessary areas in your passion and keep going past go.

...In addition, remember to laugh often! Then our mouth was filled with laughter and our tongue with joyful shouting; then they said among the nations, "The LORD has done great things for them." ~ Psalms 126:2

Life Through Lasagna Eyes - remember what love feels like. That short moment of reflection helps to welcome the love that is to come!

REMEMBER! NEVER LIVE A 40/40 AND THINK THAT IS YOUR WAY OUT. YOU HAVE SO MUCH MORE POTENTIAL AND GREATNESS INSIDE OF YOU BEGGING TO BE LET OUT SO YOU CAN LIVE HOW YOU WANT!

Not how society predicts!

Index

Below are scriptures that relate to each chapter for encouragement as you as you build your empire.

Chapter One: Life in the Noodle!

Foundation

Isaiah 33:6 - He will be the foundation of your future. The riches of salvation are wisdom and knowledge. The fear of the LORD is [your] treasure.

Chapter Two: Loss and Love!

Train Your Brain

Proverbs 4:25-26 - "Let your eyes look straight ahead, and your eyelids look right: before you. Ponder the path of you feet, and let all your ways be established."

Chapter Three: The Sauce!

Enlarge Your Life

Ecclesiastes 7:12 - For wisdom is a defense, and money is a defense; but the Excellency of knowledge is, that wisdom: giveth life to them that have it.

Chapter Four: Recipes

Do Something Nice For Others

Mathew 6:33 - But seek first his kingdom and his righteousness, and all these things will be given to you as well.

Chapter Five: More Cheese Please!

Expect More ...Expect Great News!

Romans 8:28 - "And we know that all things work together for good to them that love God, to them who are the called according to His purpose"

Chapter Six: All My Children!

Let Memories Be Meaningful Layers in Your Life!

Psalm 127:13 - Children are a heritage from the LORD, offspring a reward from him.

Jeremiah 29:11 - For I know the plans I have for you," declares the LORD, "plans to prosper you and not to harm you, plans to give you hope and a future.

Chapter Seven: Laughter!

Laugh Often! A smile is as good as a laugh

Proverbs 17:22 - A cheerful heart is good medicine, but a crushed spirit dries up the bones.

Chapter Eight! To Love Again!

Let it Happen!

I Corinthians 13:4 - Love is patient, love is kind. It does not envy, it does not boast, it is not proud
The hunger for love is much more difficult to remove than the hunger for bread. ~Mother Teresa

The title of the book is Life Through Lasagna Eyes!
It is my hope that this book helps you immeasurably as it has helped me in dealing with pain that comes with divorce, tragedy, loss, and the power that comes with loving again!

Samantha Kendall

Scriptures are taken from both the King James Version (KJV) of the God's Holy Bible and New International Version (NIV).
Inspirational quotes by Samantha Kendall & Mother Theresa
www.whatchristianswanttoknow.com

Life Through Lasagna Eyes:

The Recipes for Life

Is layered with Un-anchoring the greatest hurt to finding your passion as each chapter is built like lasagna. Samantha Kendall known as Sam...The Lasagna Lady, owner of Award winning (CBS) and Best Comfort Food (3rd Annual Pastoral Artisan Produce Festival) shares her journey of how she overcame adversities and tragedy discovering her destiny in entrepreneurship.

This vibrant, heartfelt, and hilarious book is coupled with recipes to live by as Sam shares her pain and humor.

"Parents, if your children run when you cook, run with them!" ~ Samantha Kendall.

Have you ever wondered how a nation gets fed infinitely; by helping others to embrace their entrepreneurial spirit past their pain. This is the inspired pulse that God called me to write Life Through Lasagna Eyes: The Recipes for Life.

Her daughter Amanda would run and hide when she cooked for her when she was 2 years old. One of the funniest moments, she recalls! After several attempts, Sam soon learned how to prepare great meals. Although Amanda's favorite was bacon and white rice, she loved Sam's lasagna.

Amanda's siblings were in disbelief of a horrible tragedy. Shortly after Sam's ex-husband left her and the children, her daughter Amanda was murdered on Valentine's Day 2006.

Finding the strength to move forward after this heartbreak and tragedy unfolded lasagna. Before she died, she said, "Do You Ma." She knew that meant to move forward with lasagna.

Sam is currently writing the next Life Through Lasagna Eyes series to this stand-alone inspirational self-help.

Placing a pan of baked lasagna on the table for her children to eat healthier and enjoy is what built their strong foundation of resilience and faith giving Sam the vision to start her own business.

Sam's story is bundled with hope to boost everyone to soar in the face of tragedy and heartbreak to finding their passion. Looking past current conditions allows anyone to look through different eyes; Sam's is lasagna.

Sam dedicates this book to everyone that lost a loved one's through violence, their families and the many lives that are touched. She hopes this book will encourage anyone that has experienced loss or heartbreak to live beyond his or her highest pain.

In memory of Amanda Skie Gallon, Sam dedicates this book to victims of violence, their families, and the many lives that are touched on such tragic acts.

Recipes From the Heart!

"When life throws you lemon, make something delicious."

-Samantha Kendall

Watermelon Juice

with Lemon & Parsley

Did you know, according to HeathAmbition.Com, that watermelon has many benefits? I never knew all of them, but I enjoy making this tasty treat. I call it my Watermelon Juice with Lemon and Parsley. Try this tasty drink, it is filled with vitamins and is good for your heart, skin and cancer prevention. This is my version of Watermelon Juice. Although it is refreshing to drink without adding to it, I like to add a lemon and parsley leaf.

Ingredients:
1 5-6 lb. Seedless Watermelon (I prefer removing the seeds from a seeded watermelon).
1 Lemon
1 Parsley Leaf

Directions:
Slice watermelon in half; with large spoon, scoop chunks of watermelon flesh into your blender. Throw away the rind.

Blend until pulverized (usually takes about 1.5 minutes).

Over ice, pour into pitcher or into glasses. Top with slices of lemon and parsley leaf.

The watermelon yields approximately 4 tall glasses.

Spice it up and add a little crushed red bell peppers to your blender with the watermelon – it makes for a refreshing drink with a kick!

Enjoy!

Sam's Chicken Salad

Salads are great all year long! One of the salads I love to make for my family is my Chicken Salad.

Ingredients:

1 Head of Lettuce (Optional: Leaf or your choice of lettuce)

2 Boneless Skinless Chicken Breast

6 Eggs (Boiled)

3 Roma Tomatoes

½ Cup of Mozzarella Cheese

Directions:

Gently place 6 eggs in small pot. Pour cold water in the pot using only enough to cover the eggs and place over medium heat. Boil eggs until both yolk and egg white is fully cooked. Once fully cooked, pour off unused water. Carefully remove hard-boiled eggs from small pot and set aside. Cool and peel egg shells with desired method (my method: 1 tap at each end of the cooled boiled egg; peeling the tapped ends along with the remaining of the shell; discard). Slice 1/8 inch.

Pour small amount of water to cover skillet, remove chicken breast from packaging, and set in water over medium heat.

Flipping on both side occasionally, cook until fully cooked temperature of 165° Fahrenheit. Let cool, place on cutting board and slice ¼ inch thick and set aside.

Slice lettuce in half; face down and cut ½ inch thick slices. Place in large salad bowl and set aside.

Using a separate cutting board for slicing your tomatoes, remove the core, cut in half, face down and slice (keep the pointed part of the knife down on the table). Set aside

Add tomato and egg slices on top of lettuce; add cooked chicken on top of tomato and eggs. Sprinkle mozzarella cheese over salad and serve!

Enjoy!

Spaghetti Night with Family

Spice up your family night with cooking, fun, and love! One thing I love more is spending quality time with family and friends! One way I express my love is cooking. Something you love to do and are passionate about is the perfect balance in your life. Below is the way I make my spaghetti.

Ingredients:

1.5 to 2 lbs. of boxed Spaghetti (Optional: Fresh Spaghetti)

1 Pound of Ground Turkey (Optional: Ground Beef)

¼ Cup Water

4 Tablespoons Extra Virgin Olive Oil

1 Medium Orange Bell Pepper

1 Medium Red Bell Pepper

1 Medium Green Bell Pepper

2 Teaspoons Dried Basil

2 Teaspoons Lavender

2 Teaspoons Oregano

1 Pinch Crushed Red Pepper

1 Tablespoon Ground Black Pepper

45 oz. of your favorite Spaghetti Sauce

1.5 Cups of Parmesan Cheese

Spice it up by adding 3 Pinches of Crushed Red Pepper

Directions:

Combine Basil, Lavender, and Oregano and set aside. In a large skillet, add extra virgin olive oil. Heat skillet medium and add the bell peppers. Dash ½ of the combined seasonings onto the bell peppers and sauté to slightly soft and set aside.

In a separate skillet, place ¼ cup water, ground turkey in skillet, and add the remaining seasonings, cook, and stir until meat is brown or fully cooked.

Meat sauce:

Pour fully cooked ground turkey into a cooking pot, stir in your favorite spaghetti sauce. Add sautéed bell pepper and Parmesan cheese on low heat. Cook until Parmesan cheese is well blended with meat and sauce.

Prepare spaghetti noodles as instructed on box and set aside once it is cooked.

In your favorite decorative bowl, place cooked spaghetti noodles on bottom and lay the meat sauce on top. Sprinkle with ground black pepper and enjoy!

Try My Award Winning Chilli Dish

Black Bean BBQ Chili Lasagna

with Sweet Italian Turkey Sausage

Ingredients:

3 10x10 Lasagna Pasta Sheets (fresh)

4 Sweet Italian Turkey Sausage (optional)

3 Tbsp. BBQ Sauce (your choice)

1½ Cups of Shredded Cheddar Cheese

1½ Cups of Shredded Mozzarella Cheese

1/3 Cup of cold water

Bean Mixture:

1-15 oz. Can Black Beans

1-15 oz. Can of Kidney Beans

1 Pkg. Chili Seasoning

1 Tbsp. Yellow Mustard

1½ Tbsp. Light Brown Sugar

1½ Cups of BBQ Sauce

Chopped white and green onion

Spice it up by replacing the Sweet Italian Turkey Sausage with a fiery hot Italian Sausage and some Sriracha Sauce.

Directions:

Preheat oven to 375.

In a large bowl, gently fold all bean mixture ingredients together. Cover and set to the side.

Fill ½ aluminum pan with 1/3 cup of cold water. Place sweet Italian sausage in pan and cover with aluminum foil. Cook in oven at 375 degrees for 1 hr. (or until done). Carefully remove from oven and let cool under cold running water. Cut sausage lengthwise ¼ inch thick and set to the side.

Secure 1 full size-baking pan (lasagna pan optional).

Coat the bottom of pan with 3 Tbsp. of BBQ Sauce. Lay in one pasta sheet of Lasagna (trim sides to fit pan). From Bean Mixture, coat lasagna sheet with 1/3 of the mixture evenly. Layer in two sausages on an angle (/) on top of bean mixture. Spread 1½ cups of mozzarella cheese evenly to cover completely.

Repeat layer process, this time adding Cheddar Cheese. Place the last pasta noodle on top and trim to pan size. Cover noodle with remaining bean mixture.

Cover pan with aluminum foil and place in the oven for 18-20 min (or until cheese is melted).

Carefully remove from oven and allow cooling time. Sprinkle chopped white and green onions on top (optional).

Double ingredients for larger pan sizes.

Cheers and Enjoy!!